Vocal Selections

INTO THE WOODS

Music and Lyrics by
Stephen Sondheim

Book by
James Lapine

SCENES FROM THE ORIGIN

BROADWAY PRODUCTION

PHOTOGRAPHS
BY
MARTHA
SWOPE

STEPHEN SONDHEIM
wrote the music and lyrics for *Sunday In The Park With George* (1984), *Merrily We Roll Along* (1981), *Sweeney Todd* (1979), *Pacific Overtures* (1976), *A Little Night Music* (1973), *The Frogs* (1974), *Follies* (1971), *Company* (1970), *Anyone Can Whistle* (1964) and *A Funny Thing Happened On The Way To The Forum* (1962), as well as the lyrics for *Do I Hear A Waltz?* (1965), *Gypsy* (1959) and *West Side Story* (1957), and additional lyrics for *Candide* (1973). *Side By Side By Sondheim* (1976), *Marry Me A Little* (1981) and *You're Gonna Love Tomorrow* (originally presented as *A Stephen Sondheim Evening* on March 3, 1983) are anthologies of his work as composer and lyricist. He composed the film scores for *Stavisky* (1974) and *Reds* (1981), songs for a television production, *Evening Primrose* (1966), and co-authored the film *The Last of Sheila*. He provided incidental music for Broadway's *Twigs* (1971), *Girls of Summer* (1956) and *Invitation To A March* (1961). He won Tony Awards as Best Composer and Lyricist for *Sweeney Todd, A Little Night Music, Follies* and *Company*. All of these musicals won

the New York Drama Critics' Circle Award, as did *Pacific Overtures* and *Sunday In The Park With George*, the latter also receiving the Pulitzer Prize in 1985. Mr. Sondheim was born and raised in New York City and graduated from Williams College, winning the Hutchinson Prize for Music Composition. After graduation he studied theory and composition with Milton Babbitt. He is on the council of the Dramatists Guild, the national association of playwrights, composers and lyricists, having served as its president from 1973 to 1981, and was elected to the American Academy and Institute of Arts and Letters in 1983.

CONTENTS

INTO THE WOODS

Music and Lyrics by
STEPHEN SONDHEIM

In - to the woods to Grand-moth-er's house ...   In - to the woods to Grand-moth-er's house...

In - to the woods and down the dell. The path is straight, I know it well.

In - to the woods, and who can tell What's wait - ing on the jour - ney?

In - to the woods, a - long the stream, A - round be - yond the li - ly pond,

In - to the woods to Grand - moth - er's house ...

In - to the woods to Grand - moth - er's house ... The

way is clear, The light is good, I have no fear, Nor

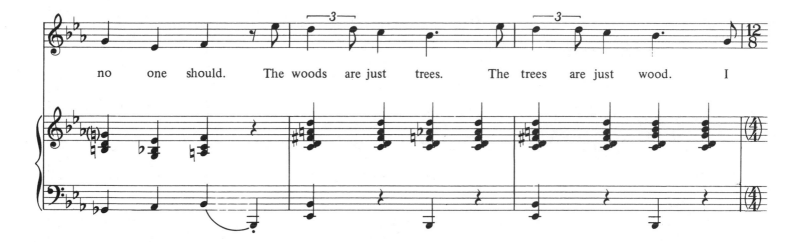

no one should. The woods are just trees. The trees are just wood. I

sort of hate to ask it, But do you have a bas - ket? *(Instrumental)*

AGONY

Music and Lyrics by
STEPHEN SONDHEIM

A La Barcarolle (♩. = 52)

p   *sempre legato*

(CINDERELLA'S PRINCE:)

Did I a-buse her or show her dis-dain? Why does she run from me?___

___ If I should lose her, how shall I re-gain The

heart she has won from me? ___ Ag - o - ny! ___

Be - yond pow - er of speech! When the one thing you

want Is the on - ly thing out of your reach.

(RAPUNZEL'S PRINCE:)

High in her tow - er, She sits by the ho - ur, main -

tain - ing her hair, Blithe and be - com - ing And

fre - quent - ly hum - ming a Light - heart - ed air. Ah. _____

Ag - o - ny!_ Far more pain - ful than yours! When you know she would

go with you_ If there on - ly were doors.

IT TAKES TWO

Music and Lyrics by
STEPHEN SONDHEIM

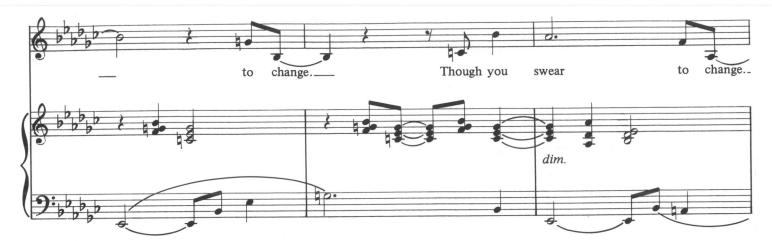

to change.___ Though you swear to change..

dim.

(WIFE:)

mp

You've

p

Who can tell if you do?___ It takes two.

changed, you're thriv - ing. There's some-thing a - bout the woods.

mp

R.H.

L.H.

R.H.

cresc.

Not just sur - viv - ing, You're

blos-som-ing in the woods. At home I'd

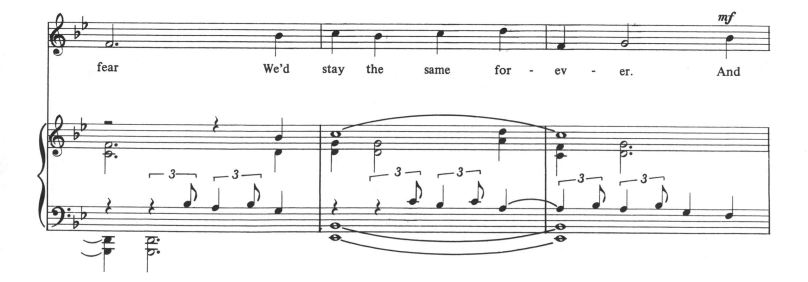

fear We'd stay the same for - ev - er. And

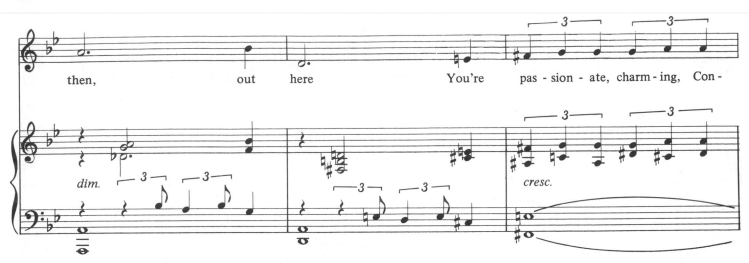

then, out here You're pas - sion - ate, charm - ing, Con -

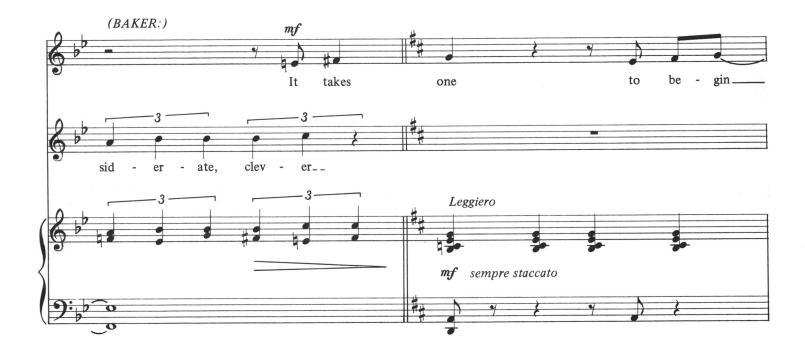

(BAKER:)

It takes one to be - gin___

sid - er - ate, clev - er__

Leggiero

___ But then once_ you've be - gun,___ It takes two of you._ It's no

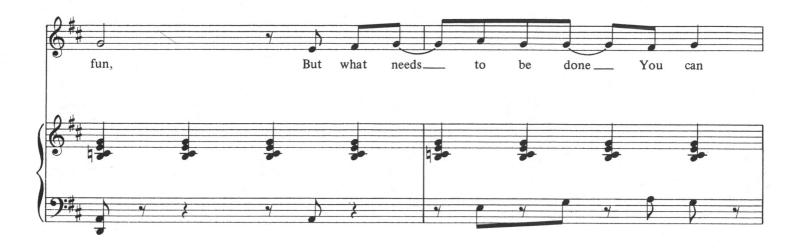

fun,   But what needs___ to be done___ You can

do,   When there's two___ of you.___ If I

dare,   It's be - cause___ I'm be - com - ing a - ware___

of us___ As a pair of us.___

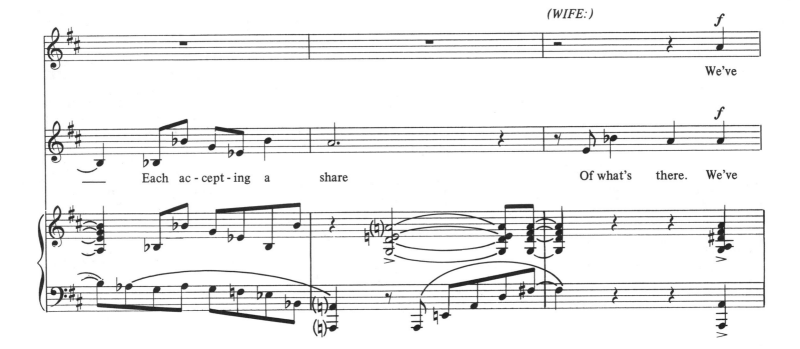

(WIFE:)

Each ac - cept - ing a share Of what's there. We've

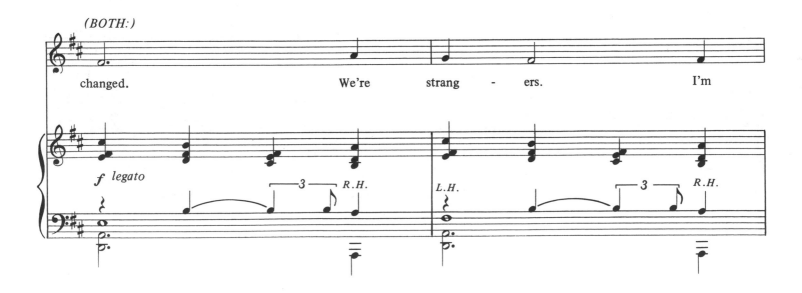

(BOTH:)

changed. We're strang - ers. I'm

meet-ing you in the woods._____ Who

minds what dan - gers? I know we'll get past the woods._____

(WIFE:) And once we're past, Let's

(BAKER:) And once we're past, Let's

dim.

hope the chang - es last Be - yond

dim.

hope the chang - es last Be - yond

(BOTH:)

mp

woods, Be - yond witch - es and slip - pers and

mp leggiero, non staccato

hoods, Just the two of us, Be - yond

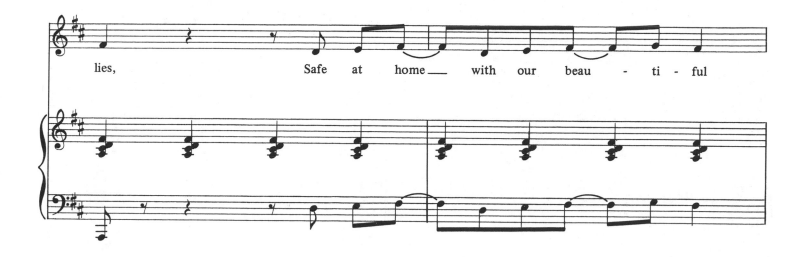

done. We want four, ____ We had none, ____ we've got

three. We need one. ____ It takes

two. ____

STAY WITH ME

Music and Lyrics by
STEPHEN SONDHEIM

Larghetto
(♩ = 100)

staccato ma pesante
mf

(WITCH:)
mf

What did I clear-ly say?___ Chil-dren must lis-ten!

What were you not to do?___ Chil-dren must see! And

learn! Why could you not o-bey?___ Chil-dren should lis-ten.___

non staccato

32

What have I been to you?_ What would you have me be?_ Hand-some like a

prince? Ah, but I am old, I am ug - ly, I em-

bar - rass you. You are a - shamed of me!___ You are a - shamed. You don't un - der-

stand.

33

Don't you know what's out there in the world? Some-one has to shield you from the

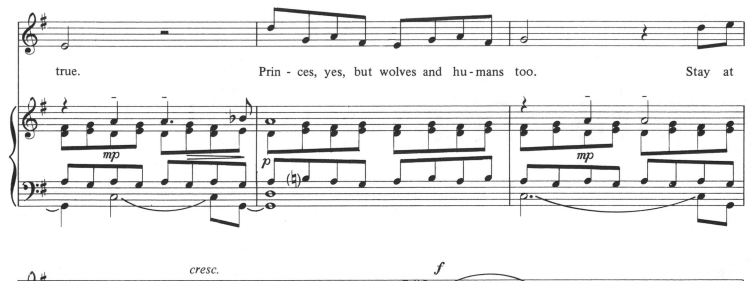

world. Stay with me. _____ Prin-ces wait there in the world, it's

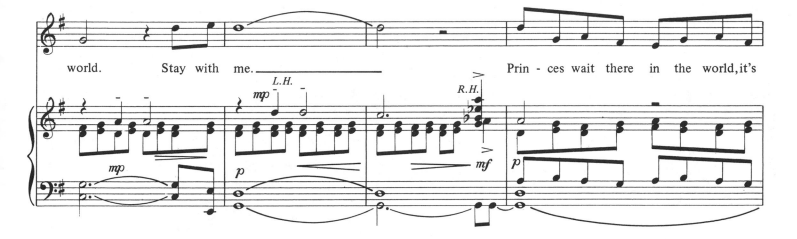

true. Prin-ces, yes, but wolves and hu-mans too. Stay at

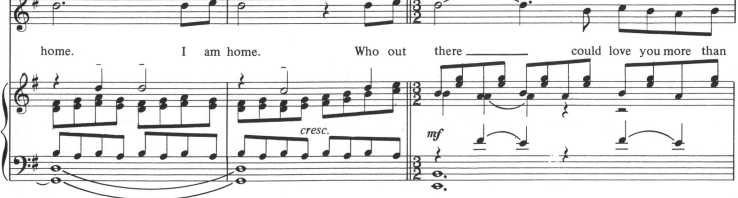

home. I am home. Who out there _____ could love you more than

I?   What out there____ that I can-not sup-ply?   Stay with

me._____   Stay with me, the world is dark and

wild._____   Stay a child while you can be a

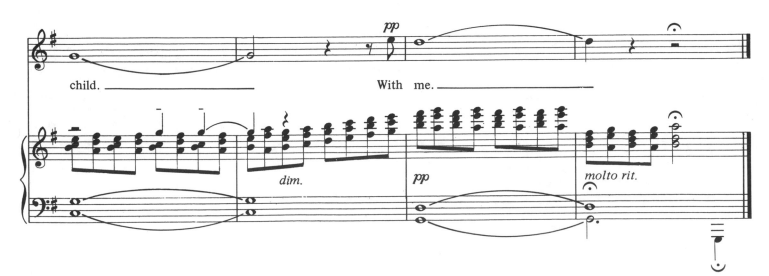

child._____   With me._____

ANY MOMENT

Music and Lyrics by
STEPHEN SONDHEIM

An-y-thing can hap-pen in the woods. May I kiss you? An-y mo-ment we could be crushed. Don't feel rushed.

Once a-gain, please. Let your hes - i - ta - tions be hushed.

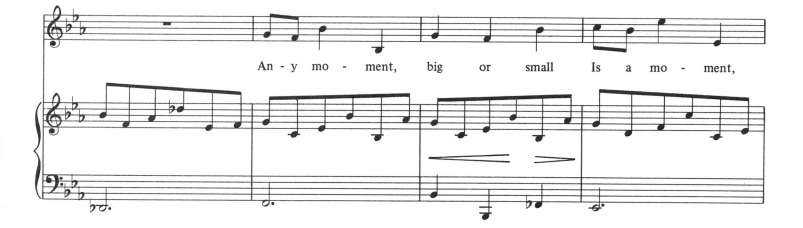

An - y mo - ment, big or small Is a mo - ment,

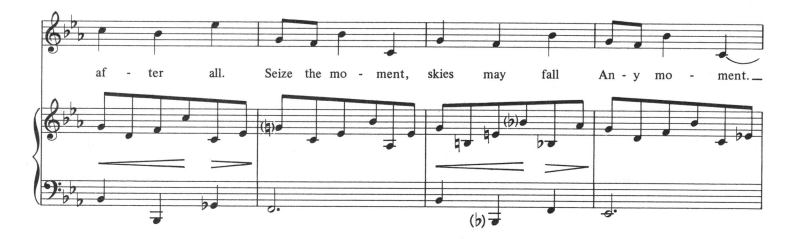

af - ter all. Seize the mo - ment, skies may fall An - y mo - ment.__

Days are made of

mo - ments. All are worth ex - plor - ing. Man - y kinds of

mo - ments, None is worth ig - nor - ing. All we have are

mo - ments, Mem - o - ries for stor - ing. One would be so

bor - ing ...

Right and wrong don't hap-pen in the woods, on - ly feel - ings. Let us meet the mo - ment un - blushed. Life is of - ten so un - pleas - ant. You must know that,

as a peas - ant. Best to take the mo - ment pres - ent As a pres - ent

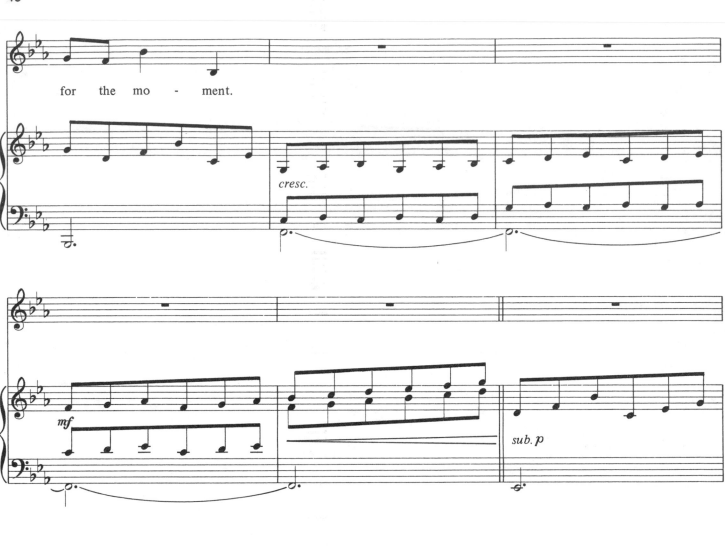

for the mo - ment.

This was just a mo - ment in the

woods, Our mo - ment, Shim - mer - ing and

love - ly and sad. Leave the mo - ment,

just be glad For the mo - ment that we had. Ev - 'ry mo - ment

is of mo - ment When you're in the woods. ____

dim.

pp

NO MORE

Music and Lyrics by
STEPHEN SONDHEIM

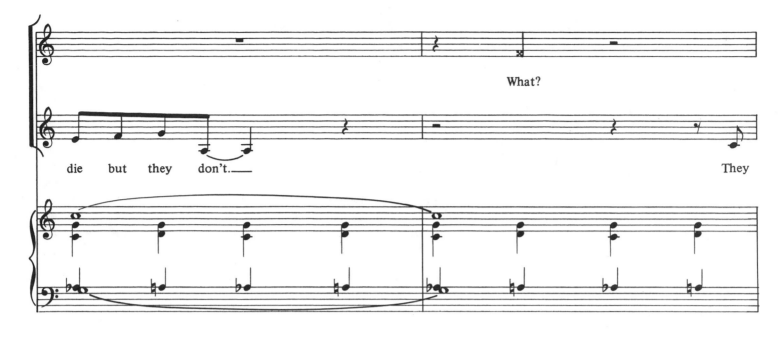

die but they don't.___ They

dis - ap - point in turn, I fear, For - give, though, they won't.___

poco rall.

No more

BAKER:

rid - dles,___ No more jests.

44

No more curs - es you can't un - do,_____ Left by fath - ers you nev - er knew.____

No more quests.

No more feel - ings,_____

Time to shut the door.

Just ... no

more.

less there's a "where," You'll on-ly be wan-der-ing blind. Just more

ques-tions, Dif-f'rent kind. Where are we to

go? Where are we ev-er to go?

Run-ning a-way,_ We'll do it.

Why sit a - round,_ re - signed?_ Trou - ble is, son,_ The

far - ther you run,_ The more you feel un - de - fined _ For

what you have left_ un - done, And more, what you've left be -

hind. We dis - ap - point, we leave a mess. We

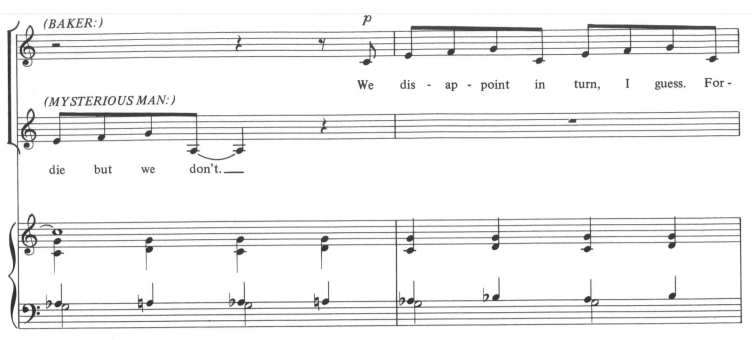

(BAKER:)

We dis - ap - point in turn, I guess. For -

(MYSTERIOUS MAN:)

die but we don't.___

get, though, we won't___ Like fath - er, like son.

Like fath - er, like son.

rit.

a tempo

(BAKER:) p

No___ more gi - ants,

the good - byes,___ The re - vers - es,___ All___ the won - der - ing what___ e - ven

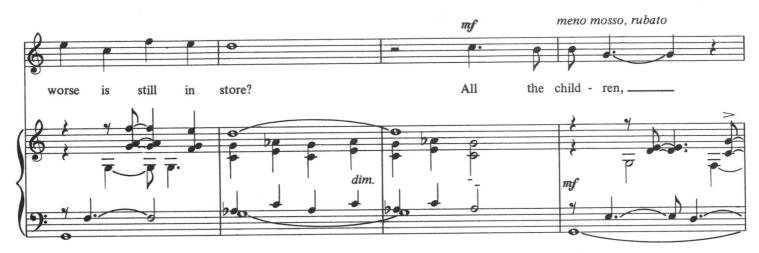

worse is still in store? All the child - ren,___

All the gi - ants ...___ No more.___

NO ONE IS ALONE

Music and Lyrics by
STEPHEN SONDHEIM

lone, tru - ly. No one is a - lone.

dim. *poco rall.*

Some times peo - ple leave you___ Half way through the wood.

p *a tempo* *marc.* *poco rall.*

Oth - ers may de - ceive you.___ You de - cide what's good._____

a tempo

___ You de - cide a - lone, But no one is a - lone.

mp

PLAYBILL®

MARTIN BECK THEATRE

CAST
(in order of appearance)

Narrator	TOM ALDREDGE
Cinderella	KIM CROSBY
Jack	BEN WRIGHT
Baker	CHIP ZIEN
Baker's Wife	JOANNA GLEASON
Cinderella's Stepmother	JOY FRANZ
Florinda	KAY McCLELLAND
Lucinda	LAUREN MITCHELL
Jack's Mother	BARBARA BRYNE
Little Red Ridinghood	DANIELLE FERLAND
Witch	BERNADETTE PETERS
Cinderella's Father	EDMUND LYNDECK
Cinderella's Mother	MERLE LOUISE
Mysterious Man	TOM ALDREDGE
Wolf	ROBERT WESTENBERG
Rapunzel	PAMELA WINSLOW
Rapunzel's Prince	CHUCK WAGNER
Grandmother	MERLE LOUISE
Cinderella's Prince	ROBERT WESTENBERG
Steward	PHILIP HOFFMAN
Giant	MERLE LOUISE
Snow White	JEAN KELLY
Sleeping Beauty	MAUREEN DAVIS